REFRIGERATOR
ART QUILTS

Preserving Your Child's
Art in Fabric

JENNIFER PAULSON

That Patchwork Place®

CREDITS

Technical Editor	Barbara Weiland
Managing Editor	Greg Sharp
Copy Editor	Tina Cook
Proofreader	Melissa Riesland
Design Director	Judy Petry
Cover Designer	David Chrisman
Text Designer	Barbara Schmitt
Production Assistant	Claudia L'Heureux
Illustrator	Laurel Strand
Illustration Assistant	Lisa McKenney
Photographer	Brent Kane
Photography Assistant	Richard Lipshay

Refrigerator Art Quilts: Preserving Your
Child's Art in Fabric
© 1996 by Jennifer Paulson
That Patchwork Place, Inc., PO Box 118
Bothell, WA 98041-0118 USA

Printed in the United States of America
01 00 99 98 97 96   6 5 4 3 2 1

Library of Congress Cataloging-in-Publication Data
Paulson, Jennifer,
    Refrigerator art quilts : preserving your child's art in fabric/ Jennifer Paulson.
        p.   cm.
    ISBN 1-56477-132-6
    1. Quilting. 2. Patchwork. 3. Appliqué. 4. Children's art. I. Title.
TT835.P389 1996
746.46—dc20   95-26024
                                          CIP

DEDICATION

This book is dedicated to my husband, Randy. Even though he has never understood why anyone would want to cut fabric apart only to sew it together again, he has been nothing but supportive of my quilting endeavors.

This book must also be dedicated to my dear children, Joel and Rachel, who made these quilts possible with their wonderful artwork.

ACKNOWLEDGMENTS

I would like to thank:

My aunt, Bonnie Hemion. She leads a busy life but always, always, has made time to inspire, guide, and support me through my projects. I must also say thanks to her for letting me dig through her wonderful stash of fabric on many occasions.

My mother, Laurie Lehman, who encouraged me to get involved with her quilt club, Issaquah Quilters. It was shortly after joining the club that I made my first quilt. I also owe my mother many thanks for her constant encouragement, which truly kept me going. I love you, Mom!

My good friends, Kerri Cerney, Lila Anderson, Lucy Nylander, Fran Jones, and my dear sister, Michelle Lehman. Thanks for your friendship.

Linda Kraus and all the wonderful women who make up Issaquah Quilters. Thanks for your guidance and for sharing your ideas and your passion for quilting!

Barbara Weiland, Kerry Hoffman, Ursula Reikes, and the entire group at That Patchwork Place. Thanks for making this possible.

That Patchwork Place®

MISSION STATEMENT

WE ARE DEDICATED TO PROVIDING QUALITY PRODUCTS AND SERVICES THAT INSPIRE CREATIVITY.

WE WORK TOGETHER TO ENRICH THE LIVES WE TOUCH.

THAT PATCHWORK PLACE IS A FINANCIALLY RESPONSIBLE ESOP COMPANY.

TABLE OF CONTENTS

WHY MAKE A REFRIGERATOR ART QUILT?

On Joel's bus, every child is smiling.

When my son Joel started kindergarten, he wanted so much to ride on the school bus, but unfortunately for him we lived just a couple blocks from school. He could only imagine how much fun he was missing, so Joel drew a school bus picture that truly captured his vision— every child on his bus was smiling. Drawing the complete shape of each child's head wasn't necessary. My little kindergartner saw only beaming smiles.

Joel's artwork was proudly displayed on the refrigerator—a common meeting place for everyone in the family. The quilts in this book grew out of my attempt to preserve my children's art for all to see, rather than banishing it to a drawer after it was replaced on the refrigerator with a fresh masterpiece.

I established two rules at the start of this endeavor. The first was a commitment to accurately represent the child's art, and the second was to include the child in the process.

Accurately representing children's art can mean duplicating the entire picture exactly as it is or duplicating just a section of the picture. The original art for "Welcome to Our Home" (below) had one more house than was included in the quilt. The houses that *were* included are

Welcome to Our Home, *29¾" x 16¼", drawn by Rachel Paulson and made into a quilt by Jennifer Paulson in 1994. The border is a collection of the fabrics used to create the houses. A personalized label on the back adds the finishing touch.*

accurate representations of the original art.

It's important to remember that children often draw or paint pictures on separate pieces of paper that are meant to represent a single idea. For example, my daughter Rachel drew her grandma's face on one piece of paper and her grandpa's on another. The two pictures were supposed to go together, so we put them together to create the "Grandma and Grandpa Quilt" at right.

When duplicating a child's work of art in fabric, it is most important that the child is pleased with the result. Listen closely to the artist as you plan. Do not underestimate children's abilities; they often have wonderful ideas. Four-year-old Rachel informed me that she wanted her Grandma-and-Grandpa quilt to say "I Love You" on it. We sat down, and with some help she wrote the words on a piece of paper. I was able to transfer her writing to the quilt very effectively. Those three simple words meant so much to her grandma and grandpa, conveying to them exactly how she felt.

By listening to children's stories about their art, you can start to see what they see. Rachel drew a picture a few years back that still makes me chuckle. Before I tell you what it is, please take a guess. Concentrate on the brown circle "thingy" off to the side in the photo below. Believe it or not, it is Captain Hook of Peter Pan fame. If I hadn't taken the time to ask Rachel what she had drawn, I would still be wondering why she put a flag on top of a rock.

I encourage you to listen not only to children's stories, but also to their objections. I learned early on how important this was when Joel did not want me to include one of his pictures in his quilt. Sure, I listened to his objection, but I decided the picture was perfect for his quilt and used it anyway. A few tears later, I learned a valuable lesson.

Since you want everyone to know who created

Grandma and Grandpa Quilt, *16" x 17¼", drawn by Rachel Paulson and made into a quilt by Jennifer Paulson in 1993. Easy to assemble with simple borders, this quilt took only 2½ days to complete.*

the original art, it seems only natural to include the child's name on the front of the quilt. However, if it is difficult to incorporate the name on the front of the quilt, use it on the back.

I hope this book gives you a renewed appreciation for children's art and the confidence to turn that art into a treasure. Every project is unique, and every quilt is special because it represents a piece of the child's past. I found these projects to be exciting, not only because they preserved my children's artwork, but also because they generated so much enthusiasm in both the child and the recipient of the finished quilt.

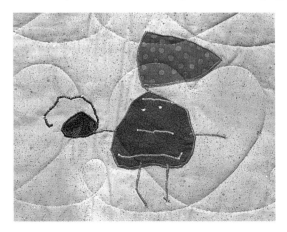

Detail of Captain Hook on Rachel's Quilt.

A BIRD'S-EYE VIEW

This book includes a variety of ideas and techniques that even the beginner can use to easily create a child's-art quilt. Before we get to the details, it is helpful to have a general understanding of the child's-art quiltmaking process. Read through this overview before you select a piece of artwork to re-create as a quilt. Then read the quiltmaking lessons that follow. The lessons include quiltmaking techniques you will find helpful, particularly if you have never made a quilt. Do not be overwhelmed. It really is easy to create a quilt from a child's artwork.

General Supplies

Listed below are the supplies you should have on hand before beginning an art quilt.

- Child's artwork
- Sewing machine with zigzag potential and a darning-foot attachment
- Freezer paper
- Light- to medium-weight nonwoven fusible interfacing
- Paper-backed fusible web
- 100% cotton fabrics for the quilt
- Assorted embellishments, such as buttons, wiggly eyes, beads, embroidery floss, and glitzy fabrics
- Cotton or cotton-polyester sewing thread
- Scissors
- White crayon or a removable marking pencil (Make sure you can remove the marks easily.)
- Rotary cutter, ruler, and mat
- 15" x 15" ruler for cutting and squaring up blocks
- Iron
- Safety pins
- Quilting needle

Step-by-Step Overview

The following steps show how simple it is to create a quilt using a child's art. The steps have been oversimplified to give you a quick glimpse of the process. Each of the steps is discussed in detail in the Little Lessons that follow, with lots of Handy Helper Tips along the way. *Be sure to read through each Little Lesson before beginning your first quilt.*

1. Select the artwork you wish to re-create and the fabrics you wish to use for each design element in the artwork.
2. Choose a background fabric.
3. Cut background fabric to desired finished size plus an extra 1" to 2" all around.
4. Place a piece of freezer paper, *shiny side down,* on top of the child's artwork. Take to a sunny window or place on a light box and trace the art. Cut outside the traced lines to make a pattern.

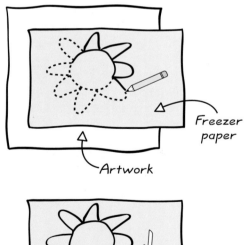

Freezer paper

Artwork

Sunshine,
28½" x 25", drawn by Joel Paulson in 1993 and made into a quilt by Jennifer Paulson in 1994. With its bright colors and smiling sun, this quilt would brighten any room in the house.

5. Place the freezer-paper pattern piece shiny side down on the right side of the chosen fabric. Using a warm iron, iron the freezer-paper pattern to the fabric.

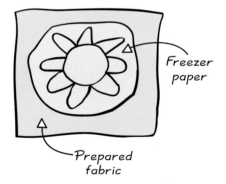

Freezer paper

Prepared fabric

6. Cut out the design shape on the drawn lines and peel away the freezer paper.

Freezer paper

7. Apply fusible interfacing to the wrong side of each appliqué (pages 15–16), or apply fusible web as instructed in "Fused Appliqué" on page 23.

8. Place the fabric shape in position on the background fabric and appliqué in place by machine. Press on both sides of the finished appliqué.

9. Add borders, layer, quilt, and bind.

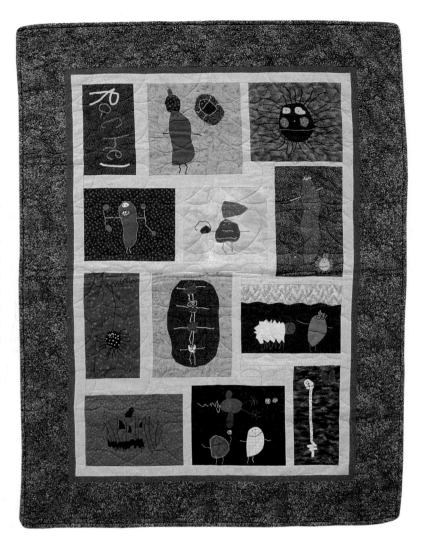

Rachel's Lap-Size Quilt,
46½" x 64", drawn by Rachel Paulson during 1992 and 1993 and made into a quilt by Jennifer Paulson in 1993. I made this colorful quilt specially for Rachel, using an assortment of memorable drawings she did when she was three and four years old.

Rocket Ships and Flying Saucers, *58" x 28½", drawn by Ryan Taylor in 1990 and made into a quilt by Terry Sargent in 1995. This was Terry's first attempt at creating a child's-art quilt, and she says that she found the process easy and a lot of fun.*

The Scarecrow, *18½" x 22", drawn by Rachel Paulson and made into a quilt by Jennifer Paulson in 1994. Plaids and a checkerboard border give this whimsical quilt a country look.*

Skateboardin' Santa, *14" x 19¼", drawn by Joel Paulson and made into a quilt by Jennifer Paulson in 1993. This drawing reveals the terrific imagination of a child. Joel decided, as I was quilting this project, that he wanted Santa to say "Joel." On a separate piece of paper he wrote his name in a creative way.*

Benjamin's Quilt, *13½" x 19½", drawn by Benjamin Polhamus and made into a quilt by Jennifer Paulson in 1994. This is a picture of Benjamin's father. If you look closely, you can see the red fingers around the arms and the yellow hair around the ears. This artwork is great!*

A View Under the Sea, *14" x 20½", drawn by Rachel Paulson and made into a quilt by Jennifer Paulson in 1994. The bright colors are a lot of fun. Made for Rachel's uncle, who has been serving in the Navy aboard a submarine for five years now.*

Pillows, *assembled by Jennifer Paulson. The* **Snowman** *and* **Teddy Bear** *pillows were drawn by Joel Paulson, and* **Christmas Tree** *was drawn by Rachel Paulson. Since these pillows do not need to be quilted, I found that I could make one in less than four hours.*

Teacher's Quilt, *32" x 43", center drawing by Rachel Paulson. Made into a quilt for Mrs. Lingbloom, Carl Cozier Elementary School, Bellingham, Washington, in 1994 by Jennifer Paulson. Members of Mrs. Lingbloom's kindergarten class traced their hands with their favorite colors, wrote their names, and voted on the fabric for the quilt backing. Hand outlines were used for the special label on the back.*

O Christmas Tree, *9" x 11½", drawn by Rachel Paulson and made into a quilt by Jennifer Paulson in 1994. Along with the buttons, the hand stitching really adds character to this quilt. This is a small project, but it was lots of fun to make in a day.*

The Best Things, *20½" x 22¼", drawn by Emily Raft in 1994 and made into a quilt by Kathleen Raft in 1995. This quilt is a collection of all the things that Emily enjoys most. Emily was so excited about being a part of the quiltmaking process that she has already made plans to start her second quilt.*

Christmas at Grandma's, *31½" x 25", drawn by Ryan Taylor in 1990 and made into a quilt by Terry Sargent in 1995. This is a picture of Ryan's grandparents' A-frame cabin. Because Ryan really enjoyed jets, he added one flying overhead.*

Jack-o'-Lantern, *21" x 18½", drawn by Rachel Craig in 1992 and made into a quilt by Bonnie Hemion in 1995. Rachel made this special Halloween picture for her Aunt Bonnie to help decorate her house.*

LITTLE LESSON 1
DEVELOPING THE IDEA

Okay, so you want to make a "refrigerator art" quilt but don't know how to develop an idea. You might start by reviewing your child's artwork and selecting five or so of your favorite pictures. Decide how many you wish to use; then ask yourself these questions:

- Who will be the recipient of the quilt?
- What are the recipient's color preferences? What is the recipient's decorating scheme? Should I use country plaids, bright primaries, or soft pastels?
- Which of these drawings best captures the look I want? Look through other quilting books, keeping an open mind for new ideas, cute borders, great fabric combinations, and even good use of space.

Noah and the Ark, *23½" x 24", drawn by Rachel Paulson and quilted by Jennifer Paulson in 1994. This was a great opportunity to use some of my favorites of the animals that Rachel had drawn over the past year. The hand-like wave adds a lot of personality to the quilt.*

- Will the quilt hang on a wall or be used and loved by a little one?

Consider making a one-block quilt using a single piece of artwork and framing it with a simple border. Many of the quilts featured in this book were made this way. Or use several related blocks to make a larger quilt. You might want to make a quilt each year, incorporating your child's artwork into a fabric memory album. What special keepsakes such quilts would be! Or re-create the art in fabric as described in this book, but instead of making it into a quilt, mount and frame it, or use it to make a pillow.

Examine the quilts throughout this book for layout ideas. You can sew several completed blocks together side by side, separate them with sashing strips, or overlap and appliqué them to a larger background.

Side-by-Side Blocks

Blocks with Sashing

Overlapped Blocks

Another approach is to ask a child for drawings based on a theme. When I decided I wanted to make the "Noah and the Ark" quilt (page 12) with plaids, the only images I needed were the ark and animals. My daughter was happy to provide the artwork to help me create the quilt.

You may find it helpful to sketch several layouts using colored pencils. This can help you select the best arrangement for the art and choose colors and borders.

It is important to take your time during the planning stages so that you like the resulting quilt. Planning helps avoid false starts and can eliminate the need to unstitch pieces you don't like. One of my biggest frustrations is getting into a project only to realize I should have taken more time to plan. I know from experience that if I don't change my mind several times during the fabric-selection process, the result probably won't be as good as it could have been. Fabrics that you thought complemented one another might look different once they have been sewn together. Be flexible and take your time as you work through the selection process.

Selecting the Background Fabric

When selecting a background fabric, remember that you want the artwork to stand out from it. It is easy to get good contrast by choosing a light background fabric for dark artwork and a dark background fabric for light artwork. I have found that a background print with some kind of movement works best. Movement gives the background personality without drawing too much attention to it.

If your background fabric has some printed motifs, it is easy to outline them with quilting stitches, thus avoiding the necessity of choosing and marking a quilting pattern on the quilt top. It's fun to outline stars, follow plaid lines, or stitch around clouds. This might be something to consider if you are a beginner and wish to make this project as easy as possible.

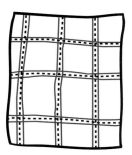

Follow plaid lines.

Quilt around clouds.

Selecting the Fabric for the Art

Normally the sun is yellow and a snowman is white, but young children have a natural sense of freedom that they often demonstrate in the colors they use to express themselves. Try to adopt this sense of freedom in your color and fabric choices. Don't be afraid to use bright colors like hot pinks and glittery yellows. Bright colors are fun to look at and easy to see against background fabric.

You may even want to involve the child in the fabric-selection process, particularly if the child will own the finished quilt. If you choose this route, be prepared to follow the child's direction. The freedom with which a child selects fabrics and colors may surprise you. You can also use this process to teach children about colors, but try not to stifle their natural creativity.

Arrange your chosen fabrics next to and on top of each other as they will appear after they have been sewn together. When you think you have the best combinations possible, leave the room for a while. When you return, you can view the combination with fresh eyes. By clearing your mind in this way, you will have a greater success with fabric selection.

LITTLE LESSON 2
FABRIC AND ART PREPARATION

After selecting your fabrics, you are ready to prepare the pieces for the block or quilt you are making. Here are simple steps that will help make your project a success.

Preparing the Fabric

Before you begin, be sure to prewash your fabrics and press out any wrinkles. Then cut the background fabric to the desired size and shape, adding an extra 1" to 2" to each side. This allows for seam allowances and a little extra room for safety's sake. Sometimes the zigzag stitching that holds the fabric in place causes the background fabric to draw up. The extra fabric allows room for this, and you can trim away any excess after completing the block.

Now you're ready to make patterns for the art so that you can cut them from the fabrics you have chosen.

Making a Pattern of the Artwork

First, decide if the art is an appropriate size to transfer to fabric. If the drawing has many tiny elements, you may want to enlarge it to make the smaller pieces easier to execute in fabric or in stitches. In contrast, you may decide that a piece of art is too large. In either case, the easiest way to adjust the size to your liking is on a photocopy machine. What better way is there to get an accurate picture in any size?

I most often use zigzag machine appliqué to attach the pieces to the background fabric. If you prefer hand appliqué or fused appliqué, you need to prepare the pieces in a different way. (See "Hand Appliqué" on page 22 or "Fused Appliqué" on page 23.)

Once the artwork is the proper size, trace it onto freezer paper. This paper is the key to accuracy in many of my quilting projects. Freezer paper, available at your grocery store, has two usable sides. It is easy to draw or write on the smooth, uncoated side, and you can iron the shiny, plastic-coated side directly to your fabric. You can remove and reuse the same piece several times for repeat motifs.

To make a pattern:

1. Place the shiny side of the freezer paper against the artwork and trace it onto the uncoated side. Make a separate tracing of each shape, allowing space around the shapes for cutting them out. Add a 1/8"-wide extension to each of the small pieces that extend from a larger shape, such as the car tires shown below. These extensions make it possible to slide the smaller piece under the larger piece.

Original artwork

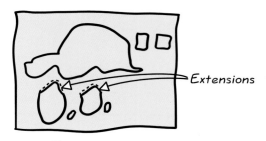
Freezer paper

If you have difficulty tracing the artwork through freezer paper, place the art on a window. Don't worry about perfection. One of the delightful qualities of children's art is the naiveté of the shapes.

2. Cut each shape out of the freezer paper, leaving a paper margin beyond the outline of each shape.

For easier sewing, you can often combine shapes when you intend to cut all of them from the same fabric. For example, if your child drew a snowman with three connected circles, you can simply trace the snowman's outline. After appliquéing the shape, use stitching to add the inner lines that you omitted in the tracing, making the snowman look like the original drawing.

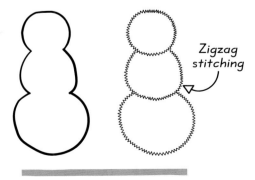

Zigzag stitching

Preparing Pieces for Machine Appliqué

I prefer to back each design piece with a light- or medium-weight nonwoven fusible interfacing. This stabilizes the raw edges of the pieces and makes it easier to stitch them in place. The interfacing tends to cling to cotton background fabrics, thus preventing shifting while you stitch. It also contributes durability to the finished quilt, which is particularly important if the quilt will be used and loved by a child. However, it will make the finished quilt top a little heavier and stiffer. Experiment with this method and with "Fused Appliqué" on page 23; then choose the one you prefer.

1. Lay each traced freezer-paper piece in place on the selected fabric. Pin in place; then cut out around the paper shape. Remove and set aside the freezer-paper pieces.

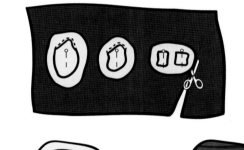

Freezer paper

Fabric cutout

If you prefer, you can hold the patterns in place for cutting by ironing the freezer-paper piece to the right side of the fabric. To remove, simply lift one edge with your fingernail and peel it away. You should be able to use the freezer-paper shape in this manner several times before the "sticky" wears out!

2. Place the fabric shape right side up on the fusible (granular) side of light- or medium-weight fusible interfacing and cut a matching shape.

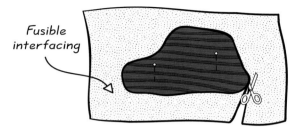

Fusible interfacing

3. Trim away 1/16" all around the interfacing shape so it is slightly smaller than the fabric piece. This prevents the fusible from sticking to your ironing board when you fuse.
4. Place the fabric shape *right side down* on the ironing board.
5. Place the interfacing on top of the fabric with the fusible (granular) side against the wrong side of the fabric.

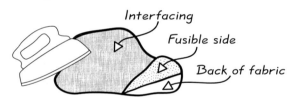

Interfacing

Fusible side

Back of fabric

6. Fuse in place, following the manufacturer's directions. Be sure to use a press cloth to protect the bottom of your iron. If you get fusible on the bottom of your iron, ask for a hot-iron cleaner at your fabric store. It removes sticky stuff in a jiffy!

Hot-Iron Cleaner

7. Reposition the freezer-paper pattern, keeping the shiny side of the paper against the right side of the prepared fabric piece. Iron in place with a warm, dry iron.

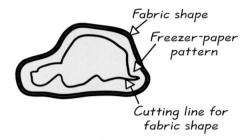

Fabric shape

Freezer-paper pattern

Cutting line for fabric shape

8. Cut out the fabric shape along the traced lines. Don't forget to include the extensions. Peel away the freezer paper.

LITTLE LESSON
PREPARING TO SEW

Now that you have prepared background fabric and all the individual fabric pieces, you are ready for the next step.

Positioning the Pieces

Arrange the picture pieces on top of the background fabric exactly as you plan to sew them. Does it look like the child's picture? Did you make good fabric choices? Would adding buttons, ribbon, lace, or other embellishments enhance the quilt? (For more information on embellishments, see Little Lesson #5 on pages 24–25.) You may want to attach some of these, such as lace, while you are sewing the appliqué pieces in place.

Don't be dismayed if you discover that some of your fabric choices don't work. I often find this to be true—one or more of the fabrics just doesn't look the way I had envisioned. It's better to discover this while you can still make new choices. Taking the time to make a few changes at this point *always* pays off!

Marking the Background

Use a removable marking pencil or sharp white crayon to mark the position of the art-work on the background fabric. This is a great way to make sure that pieces with extensions are positioned properly. I use a white crayon for marking since it irons out of fabric without leaving a trace. Be sure to test the marker on the fabric to make sure you can remove the marks later. If you use a crayon for marking and it still shows after you have completed the appliqué, place a scrap of fabric on top of the appliqué. Press the fabric to melt the crayon markings. The fabric will absorb the crayon, and it won't get all over the bottom of your iron.

Securing the Pieces for Stitching

Since each piece must be sewn in place pre-cisely, it is important to secure them in some way. There are several options. Choose one or a combination of methods best suited to the complexity of the artwork and your sewing skill.

Pinning

Use pins to hold larger pieces in place for stitching. Be sure to use thin pins to hold the pieces as flat as possible against the background fabric. You may want to try sequin pins because they are fine and short, and are easy to keep out of the way of your stitching.

Fusing

I use lightweight fusible web to hold small pieces in place for stitching. It is the easiest and best way to secure the pieces that are too small to pin or handle easily. Fusible web is available in several weights. Be sure to choose the light-est weight available. The fusible web that is easi-est to use has a paper backing. It is available by the yard and in rolls of precut strips. See "Fused Appliqué" on page 23 for instructions on ap-plying paper-backed fusible web to the pieces.

Note: Fusing can also be used with larger pieces, in which case it isn't necessary to back the fabric shapes with fusible interfacing as dis-cussed in "Preparing Pieces for Machine Appliqué" on pages 15–16.

Taping

Look for fusible tape at your fabric store. It is available on a roll with a dispenser. You can use small pieces of this tape, instead of fusible web or pins, to hold shapes in place for stitch-ing. The iron will not melt the tape. Fusible tape is particularly helpful when you are working with many pieces that have been carefully po-sitioned for stitching. Tape the pieces down so that they will not interfere with your sewing. I have also used small pieces of masking tape on occasion to hold pieces in place. However, *you cannot press over masking tape.*

LITTLE LESSON 4
SEWING THE PIECES IN PLACE

Now you are ready to permanently secure the prepared fabric pieces to the background using a technique called appliqué. In this Little Lesson, I share three ways to appliqué: zigzag machine appliqué, fused appliqué, and hand appliqué. Fusible appliqué makes it possible to add small pieces to the quilt quickly and easily. Many people prefer it because it secures the entire surface of the appliqué, including the edges, for slippage-free stitching. In hand appliqué, no stitching is visible along the finished edges of the pieces. With fused and zigzag machine appliqué, you stitch over the raw edges of each appliqué, and the stitching is visible which adds dimension.

I used hand appliqué in some of the quilts in this book. In "Dinosaurs," illustrated at right and shown in color below, I sewed the blocks

together by machine in their offset arrangement, then appliquéd the corners to the background, overlapping them in an unusual manner for additional interest.

Dinosaurs,
35" x 28", drawn by Rachel Paulson and made into a quilt by Jennifer Paulson in 1993. We have always referred to this quilt as the "Commissioned Piece," because my sister, Michelle Lehman, teaches first grade and requested a dinosaur quilt for her reading corner.

Zigzag Machine Appliqué

I use zigzag machine appliqué in all my children's-art quilts. This stitch gives finished blocks a childlike outline and at the same time quickly and securely fastens the pieces to the background to create a lasting quilt. To do this stitch, you must have a zigzag stitch on your sewing machine.

1. Thread your machine with cotton or cotton-polyester thread. Use a thread color that matches the piece if you do not wish the stitching to be obvious. To create a bold outline, select a contrasting thread. *It is best to use a matching thread color on small pieces,* because the stitches will cover the outer edges of the piece. Dark stitching makes the fabric shape appear smaller and details seem crowded.

Dark stitching

Matching stitching

2. Replace your regular presser foot with an open-toe appliqué foot so you have a clear view of what you are stitching. If you don't have this foot, check with a sewing-machine dealer. A clear plastic machine-embroidery foot is another option.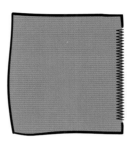

3. Adjust your machine for a closely spaced satin stitch of medium width. This stitch will cover all the raw edges, adding an outline to each piece. Test your stitch on fabric scraps to make sure it is adjusted properly and that you get the coverage you want. The bobbin thread should not show on the surface of the appliqué. If it does, loosen the top tension so the bobbin thread will draw to the underside of your work. Test the stitch again. If the fabric puckers, loosen the top tension even more. Make sure that the right swing of the needle just barely catches the outer edge of the artwork. Note the stitch width and length so that you can return to this setting easily in the future.

Satin Stitch Settings for My Machine

Stitch length _____

Stitch width _____

Stitch length too long; too much fabric shows under stitches

Stitch length too short; stitches pile up and are lumpy

Correctly adjusted satin stitch

HANDY HELPER TIP

If you have difficulty achieving the stitch coverage you want, you can stitch over the first satin stitching for a bolder, smoother outline.

4. Begin by stitching in place to lock the stitches (stitch length = 0). Then adjust the stitch to the desired length determined in step 3. Satin-stitch each piece in place, tucking any extensions under the larger pieces. If the appliqués have corners or sharp points, see the Handy Helper Tip below.

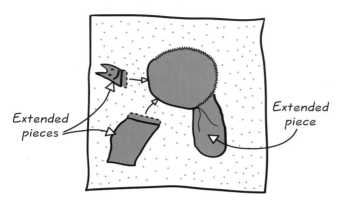

Extended pieces

Extended piece

After stitching the larger piece in place, go back and stitch around the remaining edges of the extended pieces. End by returning to a stitch length of 0; then lockstitch in place. Clip all threads close to the surface of the work.

Note: If you prefer, you can eliminate the lockstitching at the beginning and end of the stitching. Instead of lockstitching, pull the top thread to the wrong side of the fabric; then tie with the bobbin thread in a secure knot. Clip the threads close to the knot.

HANDY HELPER TIP

To stitch around corners, stitch to the corner and stop with the needle in the fabric at the outer edge of the appliqué. Lift the presser foot, pivot, lower the foot, and continue stitching.

Needle stops here before pivoting with needle down.

Stitches overlap at corner after pivoting.

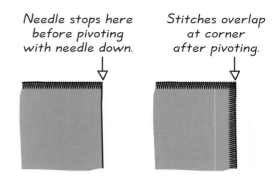

To stitch a sharp point, stitch to where the corner begins to taper. Continue stitching slowly, gradually decreasing the stitch width until you reach 0 at the point. Leave the needle in the fabric, raise the presser foot, pivot, and lower the foot. Stitch, reversing the process you used to get to the point.

Narrow the stitches gradually, reaching 0 at the point.

To stitch around curves, begin with the needle in the fabric on the inside of the curve. Move the flywheel by hand and take one stitch to the outer edge of the curve and back, returning the needle to the same hole on the inside of the curve. Then lift the presser foot, pivot slightly, take another stitch, and return the needle to the original hole. Repeat. For the next stitch, lift the needle and push the fabric forward slightly. Repeat the stitching sequence until you've finished stitching around the curve.

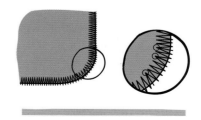

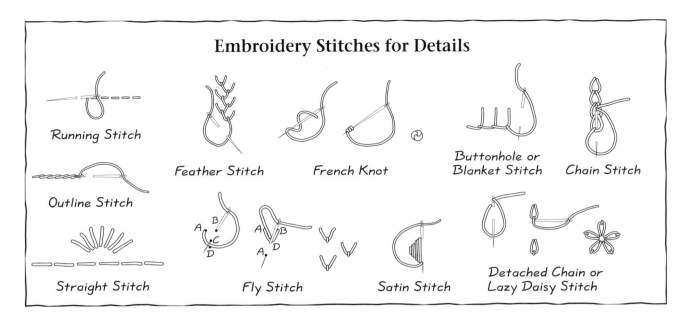

Embroidery Stitches for Details

Running Stitch

Feather Stitch

French Knot

Buttonhole or
Blanket Stitch

Chain Stitch

Outline Stitch

Straight Stitch

Fly Stitch

Satin Stitch

Detached Chain or
Lazy Daisy Stitch

Adding Faces and Other Details

If the artwork includes facial features, lightly draw them in place. Use satin stitching or straight stitching in a contrasting color so that you can see the details. For finer lines, you may want to adjust the satin stitch so that it is somewhat narrower than the stitch used to secure the pieces.

Sometimes a facial detail extends outside the head in the original artwork. Be sure to mimic this in your fabric reproduction. It is OK to stitch outside the lines, right over the satin stitching that holds the piece in place. Just select your thread colors with care. If you use a dark color to outline faces, added features that extend beyond the outer edges will not show well.

If you really want a narrow, dark outline around a face, instead of the wider satin stitch, use fusible web to secure the face to the background fabric. Adjust the satin stitch so that it takes a narrower "bite" into the shape. Because you have fused the piece down, you don't have to depend on the stitching to hold it in place and the narrower stitch won't matter.

You can also use hand-embroidered stitches, as shown above, to add details.

You can use satin stitching to add your child's name or to add details, such as arms and legs to a figure or a tail and ears to an animal. To avoid distorting your background fabric, you must stabilize it before you begin to stitch. You can do this in one of the following ways:

- Cut a small piece of lightweight fusible interfacing and fuse it to the wrong side of the background fabric where you will be stitching.

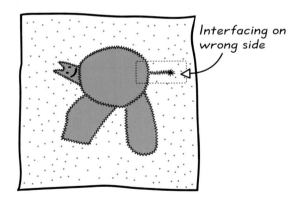

Interfacing on wrong side

- Baste a piece of tear-away stabilizer to the wrong side of the background fabric. After stitching, tear it away. This stabilizer looks like a nonwoven interfacing and is quite stiff, but it tears away from stitches easily.
- Baste a piece of wash-out stabilizer to the wrong side of the background fabric. After completing the block, tear away what you can; then spritz with water to dissolve any

residue caught under the stitching. *Do not use this method unless you are sure the dye in your fabrics will not run.*

After completing the block, use a steam iron to press it on the front and back to ease out any puckers caused by stitching. These should be minimal if you took the time earlier to carefully adjust your stitch.

HANDY HELPER TIP

If your block does not lie completely flat after pressing, do not get overly concerned or frustrated. The final step of quilting will eliminate most or all of the puckering. It will "quilt out."

Hand Appliqué

1. To make pattern pieces for hand appliqué, trace the artwork onto the uncoated side of freezer paper as described in step 1 of "Making a Pattern of the Artwork" on page 14.

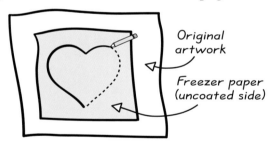

Original artwork

Freezer paper (uncoated side)

2. Cut out each pattern piece on the lines.
3. Use a dry iron to iron the shiny side of each freezer-paper piece to the *right side* of the chosen fabric. Trace around the outer edge of the freezer-paper pattern with a quilting pencil. This pencil will iron out of your fabric without a trace. (Test first on a scrap to make sure the marks will disappear.)

Appliqué fabric

4. Cut out each piece, cutting ⅛" from the freezer-paper edge on very small pieces and ¼" from the edge on larger pieces.

Cut ⅛" to ¼" away from freezer-paper edge.

5. Remove freezer-paper shape. Clip the inside corners up to, but not past, the traced line.

Clip

6. Pin the fabric pieces in position on the background fabric. Turn under the edge as you sew the piece in place, making sure to turn enough under to hide the pencil markings. To stitch, send the needle through the background fabric just next to where the thread has come out from the last stitch. Allow the needle to travel under the background fabric and then up again, catching 2 or 3 threads of the folded edge. Space the stitches ⅛" apart.

After completing every couple of stitches, make sure the appliqué is snug by tugging gently on the thread—just enough to draw the appliqué down to the surface of the background fabric. When you have stitched all the way around to the beginning point, bring the thread to the wrong side of the work and take several small stitches to secure. Clip the thread close to the background fabric.

Fused Appliqué

You need paper-backed fusible web for this technique. This product is available in several weights, from very fine to heavy. To avoid unwanted stiffness and unnecessary bulk, choose the lightest weight available.

1. To prepare for fused appliqué, trace the art onto the uncoated side of freezer paper as described in step 1 of "Making a Pattern of Artwork" on page 14. Cut out the shapes, leaving a margin of freezer paper all around each one.

Original artwork

Freezer paper

Freezer paper margin

2. Select fabrics for each shape and cut into squares or rectangles that are larger than the actual freezer-paper pattern piece. Cut a piece of fusible web to match. Apply fusible web to the wrong side of the chosen fabric, following the manufacturer's directions.

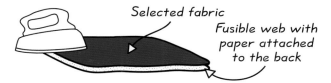

Selected fabric

Fusible web with paper attached to the back

3. Position the freezer-paper tracing with the coated (shiny) side against the right side of the prepared fabric. Iron in place.

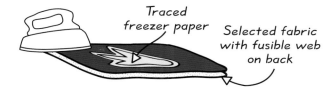

Traced freezer paper

Selected fabric with fusible web on back

4. Cut out the piece along the traced line. Peel away the freezer paper and the fusible web's paper backing. Position the fabric shape on the background fabric and fuse it in place, following the manufacturer's directions.

Peel off the paper backing.

Peel off freezer paper.

5. Add stitching if desired. Many quilters and fiber artists prefer to add satin stitching to the outer edges of fused appliqué shapes as described for "Zigzag Machine Appliqué" on pages 19–20. This provides added security for the pieces on quilts that will be laundered and adds definition to the shapes.

LITTLE LESSON 5

ADDING SIGNATURES AND OTHER EMBELLISHMENTS

The signature of the child artist is an important part of my quilts. A signature can be used effectively on the front of the quilt or on the back. Since you made the quilt to preserve a child's artwork, why not save the child's signature too?

If the child's signature on the original art is too small or too large for the quilt, you have three options:

- Use a photocopy machine to enlarge or reduce it.
- Find the child's signature in a larger size on another piece of artwork or schoolwork that was signed at about the same time the artwork was done. Trace or photocopy it.
- Try to duplicate the signature yourself, drawing it in the desired size and making sure that it is as much like the original as possible.

Signing the Work

1. Trace the signature onto the uncoated side of a piece of freezer paper that is somewhat larger than the signature.

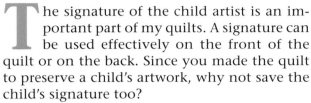

Freezer paper

2. Stabilize the background fabric, using fusible interfacing or one of the other methods described on page 17. Iron the freezer-paper with signature in place on the background fabric.

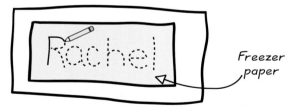

Freezer paper

Interfacing stabilizer

3. Lower the feed dogs on your machine and attach the darning foot. Lockstitch, then stitch through the freezer paper and fabric, moving the fabric in the direction needed to follow the outline. This is free-style machine embroidery. It's a good idea to practice first on scraps. Carefully tear away the freezer paper; folding and creasing it along the stitching makes this task easier. Use tweezers to grasp and remove bits of paper left behind.

After removing the paper, stitch over the name again in the same manner or satin-stitch over the first stitching for a bolder, darker signature.

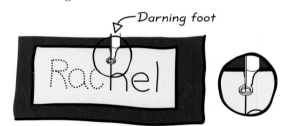

Darning foot

Other Writing

You can transfer a child's writing to the finished quilt in the same way you add a signature. Using the child's writing, you can create a special message on the front or back of the quilt, addressing it to the person who will receive the finished quilt. A short message, such as "I love you, Mom and Dad," is one option. Or maybe you have a story to tell, as we did in "Jonah and the Whale" on page 27.

The quilt that my daughter made for her teacher was enhanced with the string of pearls we added around Mrs. Lingbloom's neck. Rachel and I looked through many kinds and colors of pearls before selecting the ones she thought were best.

Add a special message with stitching.

Use the child's writing in stitching to further personalize the quilt.

HANDY HELPER TIP

If *you are making a quilt for a baby, do not add embellishments that tiny fingers could remove and then pop in a mouth and choke on. Scratchy lace is inappropriate too.*

The writing should be easy to see on your chosen fabric. Practice using different colors of thread on a piece of the same fabric that you plan to use.

Adding Embellishments

Embellishments can really add character to your quilt. Try adding button eyes, lace, or even small pieces of shiny fabric, such as lamé. Don't, however, be limited by the traditional embellishments. Perhaps a small twig will fit well into your quilt, or maybe a feather, because that is what the young artist collects. When selecting embellishments, consider the quilt's intended use. Feathers, twigs, and some novelty fabrics do not launder well. Reserve these and other fragile additions for quilts intended as wall hangings only.

Children get a lot of enjoyment out of embellishments on their quilts. If you have a place for buttons, why not let the child select them—and even help you sew them in place. Involve the child in the process whenever possible. Not only will you both cherish the creative time spent together, but you might also spark an interest in quilting and sewing.

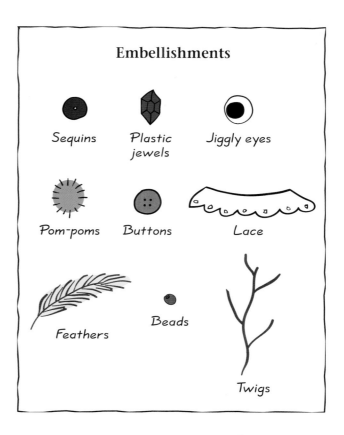

Embellishments

Sequins

Plastic jewels

Jiggly eyes

Pom-poms

Buttons

Lace

Feathers

Beads

Twigs

LITTLE LESSON 6
ASSEMBLING THE QUILT

Included in this lesson are the basic techniques you need to know to assemble your quilt. If you made a simple block and only want to add borders before finishing it, see "Squaring Up the Blocks" below, then jump ahead to "Adding Borders to Your Quilt" on pages 32–35.

Allow yourself the freedom to use bits and pieces of the ideas provided in this lesson, while coming up with a few of your own to create a one-of-a-kind piece.

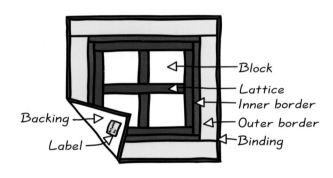

Squaring Up the Blocks

Before you square up your blocks, read through each of the following sample assembly plans and find the one that most closely resembles your quilt plan.

Before you add borders or sew blocks together, it is important to make sure the pieces are square. Use your rotary cutter, mat, and ruler to make quick and easy work of this important step. Depending on the size and shape of the block, you may want to use a long ruler or a square one.

As you trim your block, take care to keep the design centered. To do so, you may find it necessary to trim more from one side than the other. The top and bottom edges should be parallel to each other, and the sides should be parallel to each other. Check all four corners to make sure they are square.

Be sure to leave an extra ¼" of fabric all around for the seam allowances. If you plan to sew several blocks together in straight rows, make sure that all the blocks are the same size.

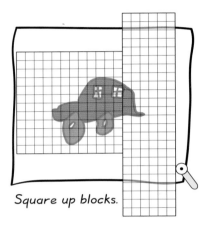

Square up blocks.

Planning the Layout

Arrange the blocks following your original plan or create a new layout. Study the sample quilt layout at left so you know the names of the pieces. Then follow the assembly directions that follow for the sample quilt that most closely matches your layout. If you wish to separate and frame each block with lattice strips, select the lattice fabric now and cut the strips.

Three-Block Quilt Assembly

The "Grandma and Grandpa Quilt" on page 5 was made using three blocks: the Signature block at the bottom, the Grandma-and-Grandpa block in the center, and the Message block on top. To assemble a similar three-block quilt, use or adapt the procedure I used to assemble Rachel's quilt.

1. Square up the Face block, making sure the top and bottom edges are parallel. Allow ¼" extra on each edge for seam allowances.

2. Place the Message panel above the Face block and shift it to the right or left as needed to center the words.

Move top panel to the right or left to center.

3. Carefully turn the Message panel face down on top of the Face block, with raw edges even. Stitch ¼" from the raw edges. Press the seam open or to one side.

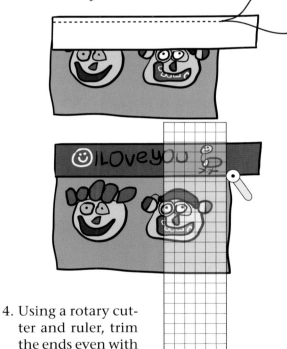

4. Using a rotary cutter and ruler, trim the ends even with the face block.
5. Repeat steps 2–4 to add the Signature panel to the bottom of the block.
6. Add borders. See "Plain Borders" on page 32.

Offset Layout Assembly

In "Jonah and the Whale" the Picture and Story blocks were arranged and sewn together in horizontal rows. First I made the Picture blocks, added borders, and planned the arrangement. Then I made the Story blocks.

Jonah and the Whale, *33¾" x 49¼", drawn by Rachel Paulson and made into a quilt by Jennifer Paulson in 1994. Although it took a while to transfer the story, the actual assembly of the quilt was easy. Notice the border treatment, a fun way to include the checkerboard pattern I love so much.*

1. Square up the Picture blocks so that they are all the same size.
2. Add a narrow border to each side of each Picture block. Cut all border strips the same width. Add borders to the long sides of the block first, then to the short sides. Press the seams toward the border strips

3. Arrange the Picture blocks with raw edges touching. Leave room for the Story panels. By simply moving the center block to the right or left you will shorten or lengthen the space for the Story panel.

4. With all 3 blocks positioned as desired, measure the width and length of the space that is left for each Story panel. Add 2" to each measurement and use the resulting measurements to cut oversized Story panels from the desired background fabric(s).

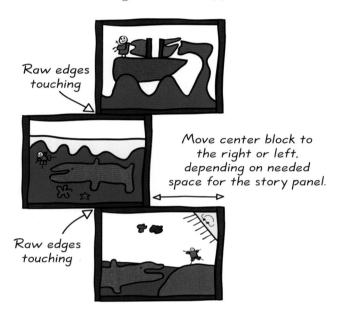

Raw edges touching

Move center block to the right or left, depending on needed space for the story panel.

Raw edges touching

5. Stitch the story on the background fabric, following the directions for "Other Writing" on pages 24–25. Press each of the completed Story blocks.

6. Center the words when you square up a Story block. Trim to the original dimensions determined in step 4, *allowing ¼" extra on the edge that you will sew to the Picture block.*

7. Arrange the completed Story blocks with the Picture blocks. Sew each Story panel to its

Picture block, using a ¼"-wide seam. Press the seam toward the darker fabric.

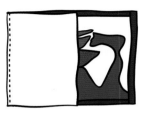

A great fish swallowed Jonah and kept him in his tummy for days

After the fish spit Jonah out he went to tell others about God.

8. Sew the rows together and press the seams toward the darker fabric.

9. Add the inner and outer borders. See "Plain Borders" on page 32.

Jonah had thought that he escaped from God until he was thrown overboard

A great fish swallowed Jonah and kept him in his tummy for days

After the fish spit Jonah out he went to tell others about God.

Simple Sashed Quilt Assembly

One of the easiest ways to arrange a group of blocks of the same size is in a side-by-side setting, illustrated on page 12. Adding sashing strips between the blocks helps to frame each block. If your blocks are a variety of sizes, see the directions for "Random-Sized Blocks Quilt Assembly" on pages 30–31.

1. Before you square up your blocks for a sashed, side-by-side setting, remember that the art in some of the blocks may take up more room than the others in one or both directions. If that is the case, select the block that is the "fullest" and square it up first. Don't forget to include a ¼"-wide seam allowance on each side of the block. Square and size all blocks to match the cut dimensions of the first squared block.
2. Lay out all your quilt blocks on the floor or another large, flat surface. Then move them around until you like the arrangement. Make sure the colors are balanced so that one part of the quilt doesn't stick out more than the other areas. Try to vary the art placement in the same way, alternating full blocks with those that are simpler.
3. To decide how wide you want the sashing strips to be, move the blocks apart until you like the spacing. Measure the space and cut the sashing strips to that width, plus ½" for seam allowances.
4. You will need sashing strips to sew between blocks. For example, for a twelve-block quilt, arranged in 4 rows of 3 blocks each, you would need 8 sashing strips. Measure the length of one of your blocks and cut sashing strips of the desired length and width.

5. Sew the blocks and lattice strips together in horizontal rows. Press all seams toward the sashing strips.

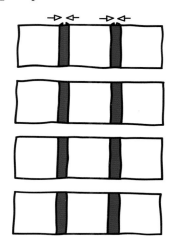

6. To cut the horizontal sashing strips, measure a completed row. Cut the sashing strips to that length and to the same width as the short sashing strips. For a twelve-block quilt arranged in 4 rows of 3 blocks each, you would need 3 horizontal sashing strips, all cut the same length and width as the first one. Sew the sashing strips and block rows together and press all seams toward the sashing. Make sure that the short sashing strips line up with each other.

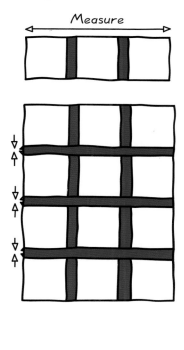

Measure

Joel's Lap-Size Quilt,
54½" x 62", drawn by Joel
Paulson during 1992 and
1993 and made into a quilt
by Jennifer Paulson in
1993. This quilt is a
wonderful collection of
twelve kindergarten
drawings of different sizes.
It was the first children's-
art quilt I made.

squaring them up so that you
don't accidentally trim away
background you really need.

1. To begin, square up each
   block as shown on page 26.
   Then arrange the blocks on
   the floor or other flat work
   surface and aim for color
   and design balance as described in "Simple Sashed
   Quilt Assembly" on page 29.
   Take your time, and when
   you think you've come up
   with the best layout, leave
   the room for a while to clear
   your mind. If you still like
   it when you return, you are almost ready to
   assemble the quilt top.

Now that all your blocks are sewn together,
turn to Little Lesson 7 on pages 32–35 to add
borders to your quilt top.

Random-Sized Blocks Quilt Assembly

You can combine blocks of different sizes
by using spacer strips in your layout. This makes
it possible to create larger units that can in turn
be sewn together. Spacer strips are like sashing,
but they are usually different widths within the
same quilt.

With this type of random arrangement, you
may need to trim down some blocks and add
spacer strips to others. Therefore, it is important to plan the layout carefully. You need to
know where each block goes before you begin

2. Arrange the blocks exactly as you want them to look after the spacer strips have been added. At this point, you might want to draw the quilt layout on graph paper to make it easier to determine how wide and how long each spacer strip needs to be. You can also check your layout at this point to make sure you can sew the units together easily in either horizontal or vertical rows or in a combination of both.

    List each spacer strip needed with its dimensions; then cut, making sure to add a total of ½" to each finished dimension for seam allowances.

3. Sew the blocks together with spacer strips between them to make larger units. Add spacer strips to the larger units, then sew all the units together. Use ¼"-wide seam allowances for all sewing. Press all seams toward the spacer strips.

Now that all your blocks are sewn together, you are ready to add borders to your quilt top.

HANDY HELPER TIP

Doing a sketch of the layout can prevent problems. I didn't sketch the layout for Joel's quilt. As I was sewing it together, I unexpectedly faced an interesting situation. As four corners were joined, a large hole was left. Not just once, but twice in the same quilt.

Rather than undo all my stitching, I solved this problem by appliquéing a fish patch over the hole. Not only did it cover the hole nicely, it also added character to the quilt—a "happy accident." My best advice is to be flexible and don't panic. Most challenges like this one have uncharted solutions.

A last-minute addition filled in the hole that resulted from lack of careful planning.

LITTLE LESSON 7
ADDING BORDERS TO YOUR QUILT

Your child has expressed creativity through artwork, and you have carefully re-created it in fabric. Now it is time to express your own creativity as you add borders to the quilt top. There are many unexplored border possibilities, so be adventuresome—just like a child.

Plain Borders

Plain borders are the simplest to make.

1. Decide how wide you want the finished border to be and add ½" to this measurement for the seam allowances.

2. Measure the length of the quilt top through the center and cut 2 border strips to this length. Pin each strip to a long edge of the quilt, easing the quilt if necessary to fit the border strip. Measuring and cutting borders this way ensures that the quilt will be "square" when completed. Stitch ¼" from the edge. Press seams toward the border.

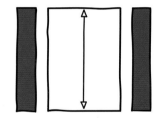

3. Measure the width of the quilt top through the center, including the side borders. Cut and sew the border strips to the top and bottom edges of the quilt top as described in step 2.

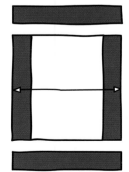

Multiple Borders

Many of the quilts in this book have more than one border. "Teacher's Quilt," shown in color on page 10, is a good example.

Notice how the narrow inner border frames the theme block, setting it off from the wide outer border, which contains the hand prints of class members.

HANDY HELPER TIP

The hand prints in the outer border of "Teacher's Quilt" make it a personalized memento the teacher is sure to cherish.

To determine how wide to cut the outer border strips, I arranged the hands around the perimeter of the completed center with inner-border strips attached.

Then I measured from the inner border to the end of the fingertip that was the farthest away from the inner border.

To that measurement, I added ½" for seam allowances, plus another 2" to 3" to ensure open space around each hand and allow for "shrinkage" caused by appliquéing the hands in place. I planned for even space on each side of the hands. It's much better to cut the strips extrawide and trim them down later.

Next, I cut and attached the outer border strips as described for "Plain Borders" at left. Then I repositioned the hands and appliquéd them in place.

"Sunshine," shown above and on page 7, has three borders. Notice that they are each a different width, creating the appearance of a matted piece of artwork. When adding multiple borders, it is important to vary the border widths for a visually pleasing composition.

Pieced Borders

The border on "Welcome to Our Home" on page 4 was pieced using fabrics in the same colors as the appliqués.

For a simple pieced border, you can cut strips in random lengths, then sew them end to end and cut them to fit the quilt top as described for "Plain Borders" on page 32.

When I made this quilt, I cut the strips 1½" wide and arranged them around the quilt, moving them until I was happy with the placement. Then I sewed them together, cut them to fit, and sewed them to the quilt top.

The Guardian Angel, *17½" x 13½", drawn by Rachel Paulson and made into a quilt by Jennifer Paulson in 1994. The plaid checkerboard border was easy to assemble and added a little extra color. It took only one day to complete this quilt.*

Checkerboard Borders

A checkerboard border, such as the one on "The Guardian Angel" above, is another colorful option. You have the opportunity to create many different looks through your fabric selection and by varying the finished size of the squares. You can use an easy strip-piecing technique to make fast work of joining the squares.

1. Decide how wide the finished squares should be and add ½" for seam allowances.
2. Cut strips the desired width (plus seam allowances) from several fabrics. For example, if you want to end up with 2" squares, cut your strips 2½" wide.
3. Sew the strips together along the long edges. Press the seams in one direction. Using a rotary cutter and a ruler, cut segments from the strip-pieced unit, *cutting them the same width that you cut the strips.*

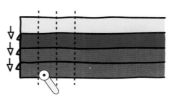

4. For a simple checkerboard border, sew the segments together end to end as shown and arrange them around the quilt top. Sew them to the quilt sides and then to the top and bottom edges as described for "Plain Borders" on page 32, but press the seams toward the quilt top rather than toward the borders.

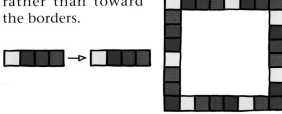

HANDY HELPER TIP

If the border strip is too long for the quilt, remove a square or take slightly deeper seams in a few places to make it fit. If it is too short, take narrower seams in a few places and remove the original stitching. The other option is to do what a child would—just cut off the excess. It won't be a perfect checkerboard, but that's OK in a child's eyes.

For a true checkerboard look, use only two fabrics to make the strip unit. Sew them together and press the seam toward the darker fabric.

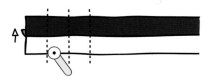

Cut segments the same width as you cut the strips and sew them together as shown, using as many segments as necessary to fit the edges of the quilt top.

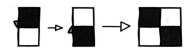

Sew the borders to the quilt top as described for "Plain Borders" on page 32, but press the seams toward the quilt, rather than toward the pieced border.

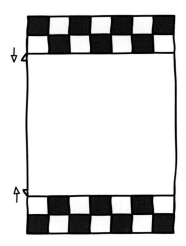

More Border Ideas

Be as creative as you wish, using border ideas in combination. For example, look at the border on "Jonah and the Whale" on page 27. I combined prints and solids and incorporated some pieced checkerboard sections to add interest and imitate a child's approach.

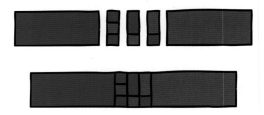

You can make fake checkerboard borders by cutting border strips across the width of a striped fabric. Look at the black-and-white border on "Noah and the Ark" on page 12 and the multicolored checkerboard border on "Joel's Lap-Size Quilt" on page 30.

For primitive checkerboard borders, check out Rachel's "Country Quilt," shown in color on page 35. The effect is wonderful, whimsical, and very childlike.

Checkerboard borders enliven each of these quilts.

Detail of **Joel's Lap-Size Quilt**, *page 30.*

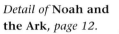

Detail of **Noah and the Ark**, *page 12.*

Detail of **Jonah and the Whale**, *page 27.*

Country Quilt, *26½" x 19¼", drawn by Rachel Paulson and quilted by Jennifer Paulson in 1993. This was my first attempt to work with plaids. The buttons, stars, and hearts all add a bit of fun to the quilt.*

LITTLE LESSON 8
ASSEMBLING AND FINISHING YOUR QUILT

You've finished the quilt top, added wonderful borders, and are ready to finish your quilt. You will want to add a special label to the back of the quilt. There are several ways to do this, so before you assemble your quilt, I suggest you go on to Little Lesson 9 on pages 40–42 and decide how you wish to make and add your label. Then return to Little Lesson 8 to learn about batting, backing, and quilting.

Getting Ready to Quilt

A quilt is made of three layers: the quilt top, a filler called batting, and a backing fabric.

Quilt top
Batting
Backing

The quilting is done through all three of these layers to hold them together, and the outer edges are finished with binding.

Batting

To begin, you need to purchase batting. Ask for low- or medium-loft batting. It's easier to quilt through these than through thicker ones. A low-loft batting is particularly appropriate for small quilts that will hang on the wall. I prefer polyester batting because it doesn't require as much quilting as the cotton battings do. It's easy to machine quilt too.

Backing

Why not let the young artist who inspired the quilt help you select the fabric for the quilt backing? It's a wonderful way to involve a child in the quiltmaking process. If the child selects a crazy, wild-looking print, go with it, even if it clashes. In the years ahead, you may both get a good chuckle out of it.

If the intended recipient of the quilt has a particular interest or hobby, you may want to have a little fun with the backing selection. My brother is in the Navy, so when my daughter created a quilt for him, we chose a red-white-and-blue print for the back.

Making a Quilt Sandwich

1. Cut the backing fabric 2" larger all around than the completed quilt top. Lay it on a flat surface with the right side of the backing fabric against the floor. Smooth out any wrinkles. The backing fabric must lie smooth and flat during the remaining steps to avoid unsightly puckers.
2. Cut a piece of batting the same size as the backing fabric. Center it on top of the backing and smooth out any wrinkles.
3. Carefully center your pressed quilt top on top of the batting. Batting and backing should extend evenly all around the top.
4. Use small safety pins to hold all three layers together. Work from the center out and place pins a hand's width or less apart. Use enough pins to hold the layers securely, but do not pin where it will interfere with your stitching. Of course, you can easily remove a pin if it gets in the way.

Backing
Batting
Safety pins

Quilting

You're ready to quilt. Since most children's-art quilts are small, it is easy to machine quilt them. Of course, you can quilt them by hand if you wish. Directions follow for machine quilting around the shapes and in the background and borders.

To quilt around design shapes:

1. Replace the presser foot with a quilting or darning foot if one of these is available for your machine. Drop the feed dogs and adjust the machine for a balanced straight stitch. If you have never done free-motion stitching (with feed dogs down), practice first on a small quilt sandwich made from fabric scraps and batting. For more information on how to machine quilt, see *Machine Quilting Made Easy* by Maurine Noble, published by That Patchwork Place.

HANDY HELPER TIP

If you are working on a large quilt, you may find it easier to fold or roll the quilt from one side to the center so it is easier to handle at the machine. Work from the center out to the unrolled edge. Then roll the quilted portion to the center and work from the center out to quilt the remainder. This method prevents quilting accidents— like catching a corner underneath your quilting.

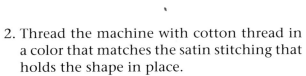

2. Thread the machine with cotton thread in a color that matches the satin stitching that holds the shape in place.
3. Stitch around the shape, outlining it with quilting. Keep all stitching outside the satin stitching.

HANDY HELPER TIP

If you wish, you can stitch ¼" away from the shape rather than right alongside it. In that case, use thread that matches the color of the background fabric.

To quilt the background:

1. Decide just how you are going to quilt the background areas of your quilt. If the fabric has stripes, it's easy to quilt following the stripes. It's also easy to quilt around printed shapes in fabrics, such as clouds and stars. Experiment with different colors of thread for a different appearance.

2. To quilt the background areas, adjust the machine and use free-motion quilting as described above for quilting around design shapes. Use matching or contrasting thread, depending on the desired effect. If you are a new quilter, I suggest using matching thread to hide less-than-perfect stitching.

When the background fabric does not have a distinct pattern to follow for quilting, consider the following alternatives:

● *Use masking tape as a guide. Stitch alongside the edges, then remove the tape.*

Masking tape

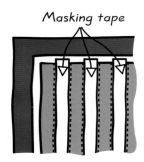

● *Use a quilting design stencil (available at your favorite quilt shop) and a marking pencil or chalk to mark a design in the background areas.*
● *Use a removable marking pencil to draw a free-form quilting pattern of your own design on the quilt top.*

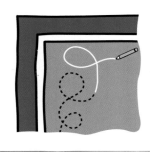

To quilt the borders:

Stitch in-the-ditch of border seams. You may also want to quilt a design in wider borders.

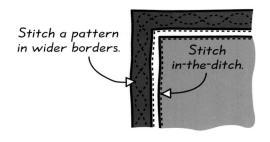

Stitch a pattern in wider borders.

Stitch in-the-ditch.

Adding the Binding

1. Trim the batting and backing even with the quilt edge.
2. Using a rotary cutter, mat, and ruler, cut enough 2¼"-wide strips from your binding fabric to go around the quilt, plus an additional 4" to 6" for going around corners.
3. To make one continuous strip of binding, sew the strips together on the diagonal. Trim the excess fabric, leaving a ¼"-wide seam allowance. Press seams open.

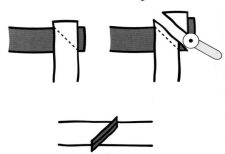

4. Turn under one end at a 45° angle and press. Trim away excess fabric, leaving a ¼"-wide seam allowance. Fold the strip in half lengthwise with wrong sides together and raw edges even. Press.

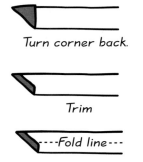

Turn corner back.

Trim

----Fold line----

5. Starting on one side of the quilt, stitch the binding to the quilt. Keep the raw edges even and use a ¼"-wide seam allowance. Start stitching a few inches from the end of the binding and end the stitching ¼" from the corner of the quilt. Backstitch and clip the threads. Remove the quilt from the machine.

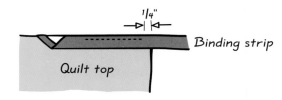

¼"

Binding strip

Quilt top

6. Turn the quilt so you will be stitching down the next side. Fold the binding up, away from the quilt.

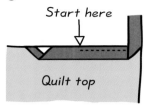

7. Fold the binding back down onto the quilt top so a fold forms at the upper raw edge and the binding edge is even with the quilt edge. Stitch, ending ¼" from the next corner. Backstitch and clip the threads.

8. Continue in the same manner around the quilt. When you reach the beginning of the binding, overlap the beginning stitches by about 1" and cut away the excess binding, trimming the end at a 45° angle. Tuck the end into the beginning of the binding. Complete the stitching.

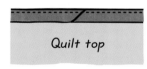

9. Fold the binding over to the back of the quilt. Sew the folded edge of the binding to the quilt backing, using the traditional appliqué stitch (page 22). The binding should cover the stitches. Miters will form at the corners.

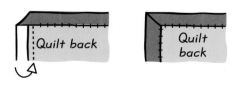

Adding a Hanging Sleeve

If you are making a wall hanging, add a fabric sleeve to the back of the quilt so that you can slip a dowel through it for hanging.

1. Buy a dowel or strip of lath at a hardware store. Cut it ¼" shorter than the finished measurement of the top edge of the quilt.
2. Cut a strip of fabric (backing fabric or muslin, for example) that is the same length as the top edge of the quilt. Cut it 4" to 6" wide (or no less than twice the width of the hanging rod, plus 1").
3. At each short end, turn under and press ¼". Then turn again and press. Edgestitch each hem in place.

4. Fold the strip in half lengthwise *with wrong sides together* and raw edges even. Stitch ¼" from the long edges to make a tube.

5. Center the seam. Press the seam open, pressing the tube flat at the same time.

6. Pin a ¼"-deep pleat across the entire length of *the front layer of the fabric tube* only.

Pin a pleat in front of sleeve.

7. Place the sleeve just below the inner edge of the binding on the back of the quilt and slipstitch in place along the top edge, the short ends, and across the bottom edge.

8. Remove pins. The pleat you released allows extra room in the sleeve to lessen strain on the quilt and the stitching.

LITTLE LESSON
MAKING PERSONALIZED LABELS

Be sure to add a label to the back of the quilt so that anyone who examines it will know who did the original drawing. Include the date the art was done, the date the quilt was finished, and your name as the maker. If the quilt is a gift, you might also want to add a personal message to the label.

Four label-making methods follow. Use one of them or come up with your own creative ideas for a special label.

Fusible Label

1. To make a quick and easy label, fuse a piece of paper-backed fusible web to the wrong side of a piece of light-colored fabric.
2. Using a fine-point, *waterproof* permanent-ink pen, write the desired information on the label. Allow the ink to dry thoroughly.
3. Remove the paper from the back of the label. Position the label on the quilt backing and fuse in place. Be sure to use a press cloth and follow the manufacturer's directions.

Artwork by Joel Paulson — Fusible web

Record the desired information with a fine-point, waterproof permanent-ink marking pen. Write on the panel after you have finished the quilt, or write on it before you layer the quilt and quilt it. If you do this, your quilting stitches will probably go through the label, but that's OK. You decide whether you want that or not.

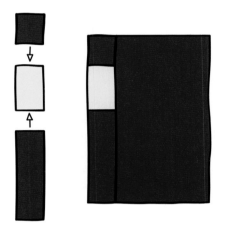

HANDY HELPER TIP

If you plan to write the information on the label before you finish the quilt, iron a piece of freezer paper to the wrong side of the panel. This will keep the fabric from wiggling while you write. After completing the label, peel the freezer paper away.

Sewn-In Label

I used a sewn-in label on the back of Rachel's and Joel's twelve-block, lap-size quilts. When I prepared the backing for each of these quilts, I incorporated a panel of light-colored fabric in the backing piece. This type of label is great when you wish to record a lot of information so future generations will understand what the quilt is all about. I wrote something about each block on the label on each of these quilts.

Child's Art Label

Consider making a label in the same shape as a part of the child's artwork.

1. Use a photocopy machine to enlarge or reduce the motif to the appropriate size.
2. Apply fusible interfacing to the back of the label fabric to stabilize it.
3. Trace the label shape onto freezer paper. Cut out the shape and use it as a pattern to cut

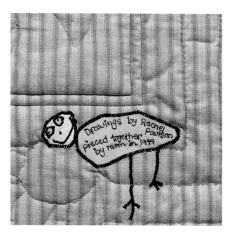
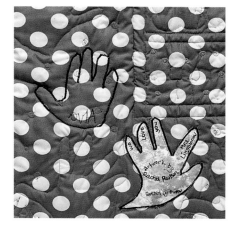

the label from the stabilized fabric. Set the freezer-paper shape aside.

4. Use a satin stitch to zigzag the label in place on the backing fabric before you assemble the quilt layers and begin to quilt. Make sure the stitches cover the edges of the label. See "Zigzag Machine Appliqué" on pages 19–20. Press.

5. Write your information directly on the shape with a waterproof, permanent-ink marking pen, or write on a piece of freezer paper that will fit inside the label shape. Position the freezer paper on top of the label and iron in place.

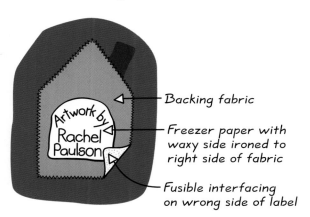

— Backing fabric

— Freezer paper with waxy side ironed to right side of fabric

— Fusible interfacing on wrong side of label

6. Stitch over the letters, following the directions given for adding signatures and other writing on pages 24–25. Carefully remove the freezer paper. Stitch over the letters again to make them darker. Press.

HANDY HELPER TIP

The more space there is between the letters, the easier it will be to remove the freezer paper. The lettering will also be easier to read.

7. If you do not want your quilting stitches to go through the label, use safety pins to secure the freezer-paper label pattern in place to remind you not to quilt in this area. If you wish to quilt the label area without stitching showing on the label, go back and hand quilt. Catch only the top layer of the quilt, the batting, and just a thread or two of the backing fabric so the stitches won't pierce the label.

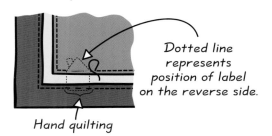

Dotted line represents position of label on the reverse side.

Hand quilting

If the artwork doesn't inspire a label, consider cutting a simple shape common to children's art, such as a heart, for a label.

Hand-Appliquéd Label

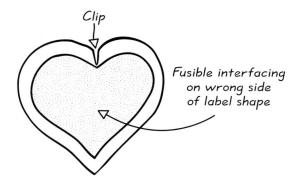

When your quilt is complete, you can attach a label by hand if you wish. This type of label will not have a satin-stitched outline. One reason to use a hand-appliquéd label is that you can add it last, after the quilt has been layered, quilted, and bound. This is probably the easiest way to make a personalized label.

1. Make a freezer-paper pattern of the desired shape. Place it right side up on the fusible side of a piece of lightweight fusible interfacing. Cut out. Next place the pattern *right side up on the right side* of the label fabric. Pin in place; then cut out the shape with an extra ¼" allowance for turn-under all the way around.

    Center the interfacing shape, fusible side down, on the wrong side of the label shape and fuse. Clip any inside corners.

Clip

Fusible interfacing on wrong side of label shape

2. Write the information on the uncoated side of a piece of freezer paper and iron in place on the label. Make sure the letters don't extend into the ¼" turn-under allowance of the label. Stitch over the letters, following the directions given for adding signatures and other writing on pages 24–25. Carefully remove the freezer paper. Stitch over the letters again to make them darker. Press.

3. Turn under the ¼"-wide allowance and press. You should be able to do this without measuring, since the fusible interfacing gives you a nice edge against which to fold.

Fusible interfacing

4. Position the label on the back of the completed quilt and use the traditional hand-appliqué stitch described on page 22 to sew it in place. Be careful to catch only the folded edge of the label and the backing fabric in the stitching.

THE LAST WORD

There! You've finished your first quilt designed by a child artist. Plan a party or ceremony to present it to the intended recipient or to hang it in a special place in your home. Then start the next one. Once your children see how much you care about their artwork, they're bound to bring you more inspiration. Who knows, you may have a budding quiltmaker or two on your hands!

ABOUT THE AUTHOR

Jennifer Paulson has had an appreciation for art since she was a child, and took every art class she could in high school and college. Pen and ink is her favorite medium—her "true love," she says. When her mother introduced her to quiltmaking in 1992, however, Jennifer set aside her pen to pursue this new art form.

As the mother of three young children, it has been Jennifer's particular joy to preserve their art in small quilts and wall hangings and to share her newfound love with friends. She says, "It has been truly exciting to see my children take such pride in their art turned into quilts. I hope that enthusiasm is passed on to our new little artist, Hannah, who arrived in September 1995."

Jennifer makes her home in Ferndale, Washington, with her children and husband, Randy.

Jennifer, Joel, and Rachel Paulson.

That Patchwork Place Publications and Products

4", 6", 8", & metric Bias Square® • BiRangle™ • Ruby Beholder™ • ScrapMaster • Rotary Rule™ • Rotary Mate™ • Bias Stripper™
Shortcuts to America's Best-Loved Quilts (video)

Many titles are available at your local quilt shop. For more information, send $2 for a color catalog to
That Patchwork Place, Inc., PO Box 118, Bothell WA 98041-0118 USA.
☎ Call 1-800-426-3126 for the name and location of the quilt shop nearest you.